KINDERGARTEN ALPHABET

Fun-filled Activities

An imprint of Om Books International

The Letter A

Write Aa with your pencil. Trace the dots first.

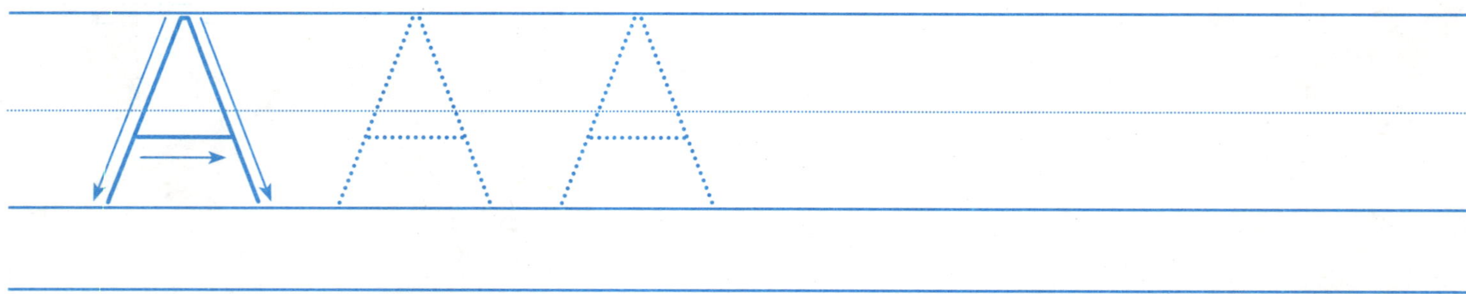

Tick (✓) all the objects the names of which begin with A.

Trace the word given below and colour the picture.

apron

The Letter B

Write Bb with your pencil. Trace the dots first.

Can you circle (O) all the objects the names of which begin with B?

Trace the word given below and colour the picture.

The Letter C

Write Cc with your pencil. Trace the dots first.

Can you circle (O) all the objects the names of which begin with C?

Trace the word given below and colour the picture.

The Letter D

Write Dd with your pencil. Trace the dots first.

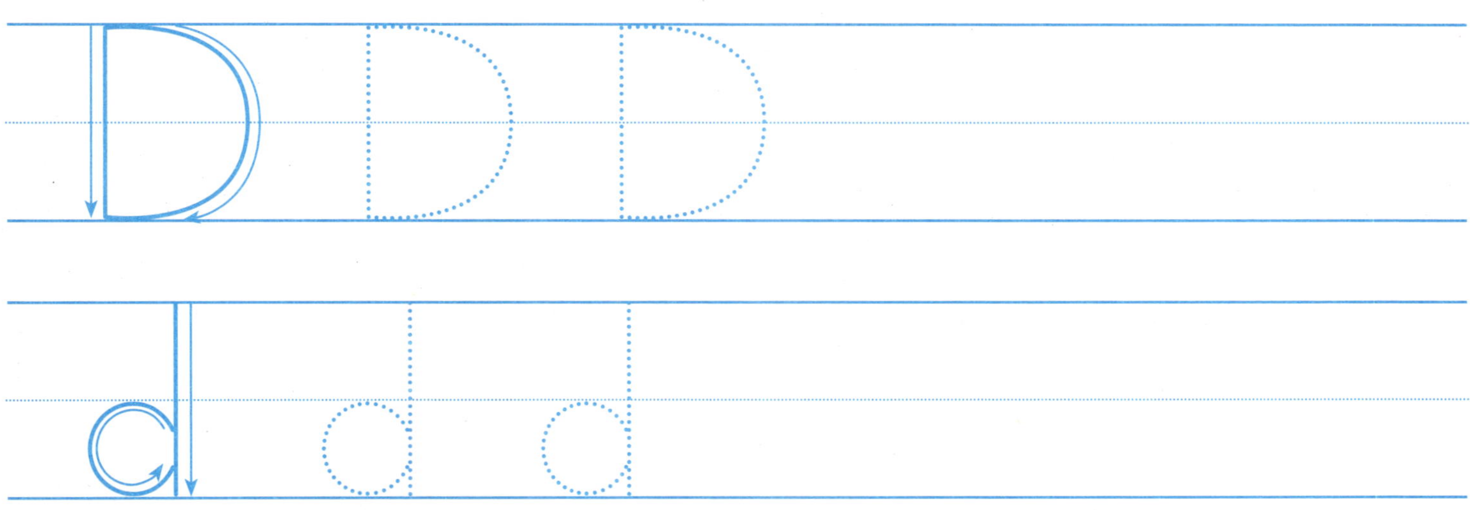

Help Din, the duck reach her home by following the objects that begin with D.

Trace the word given below and colour the picture.

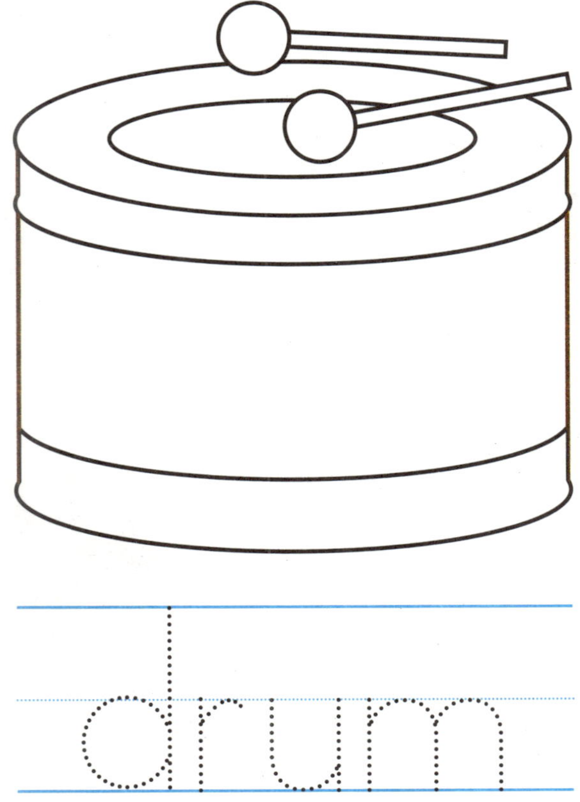

The Letter E

Write Ee with your pencil. Trace the dots first.

Draw a line from letter E to each object the name of which begins with E.

Trace the word given below and colour the picture.

engine

The Letter F

Write Ff with your pencil. Trace the dots first.

Colour the objects in the picture below the names of which begin with F.

Trace the word given below and colour the picture.

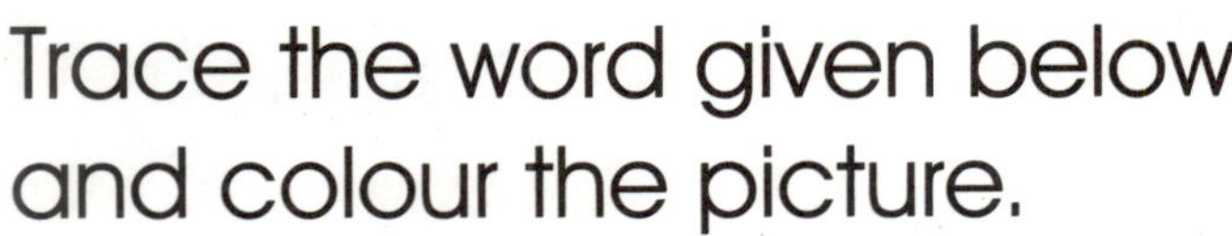

Fun With Letters

Circle (O) the objects in the picture that begin with the letters a, b and c.

Say the picture words. Circle (O) the correct letter for each picture.

A D F

E C D

B F A

The Letter G

Write Gg with your pencil. Trace the dots first.

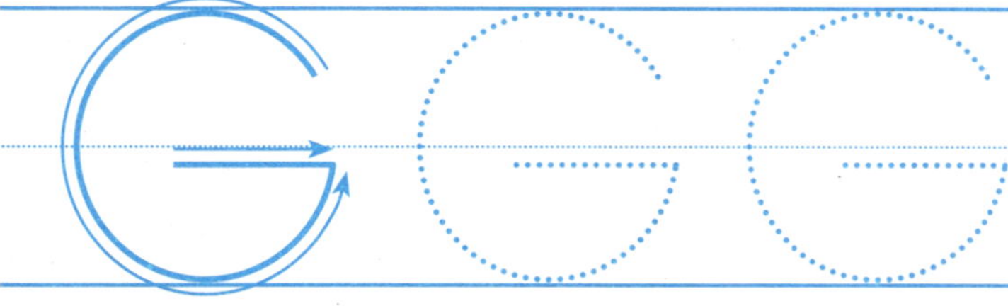

How many Ggs can you find in the picture? Circle (O) them all.

Trace the word given below and colour the picture.

grapes

The Letter H

Write Hh with your pencil. Trace the dots first.

Fill in the blanks with 'h' to complete each word. Join the dots and colour the objects.

Trace the word given below and colour the picture.

The Letter I

Write Ii with your pencil. Trace the dots first.

Circle (O) each object the name of which begins with I.

Trace the word given below and colour the picture.

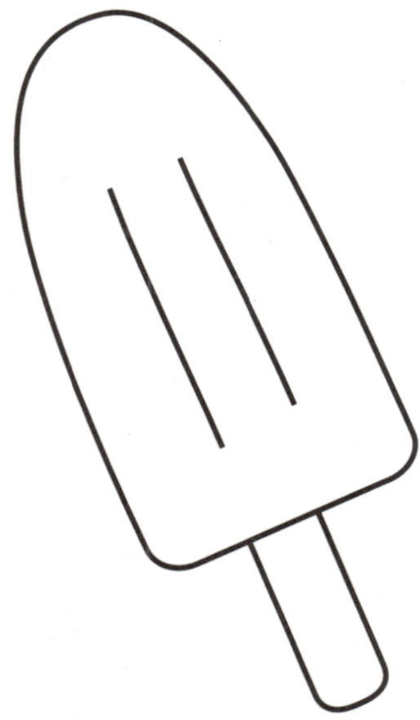

ice cream

The Letter J

Write Jj with your pencil. Trace the dots first.

Can you name all the objects in the picture the names of which begin with J?

Trace the word given below and colour the picture.

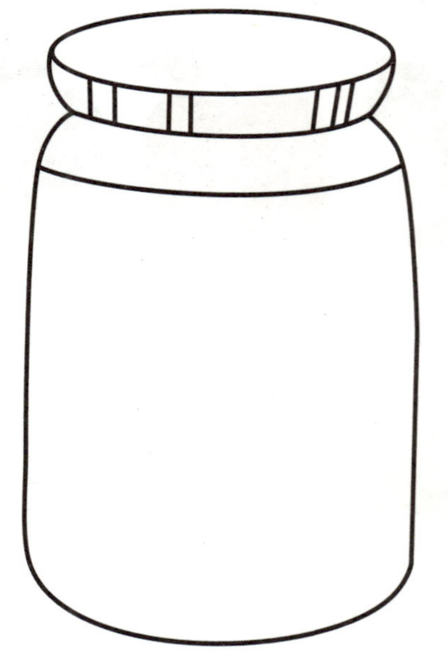

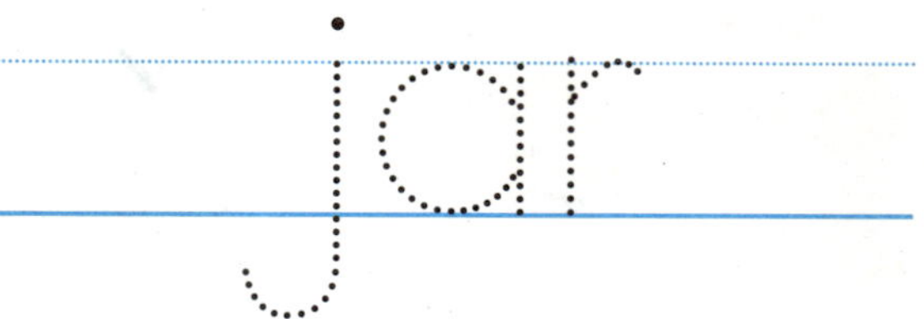

The Letter K

Write Kk with your pencil. Trace the dots first.

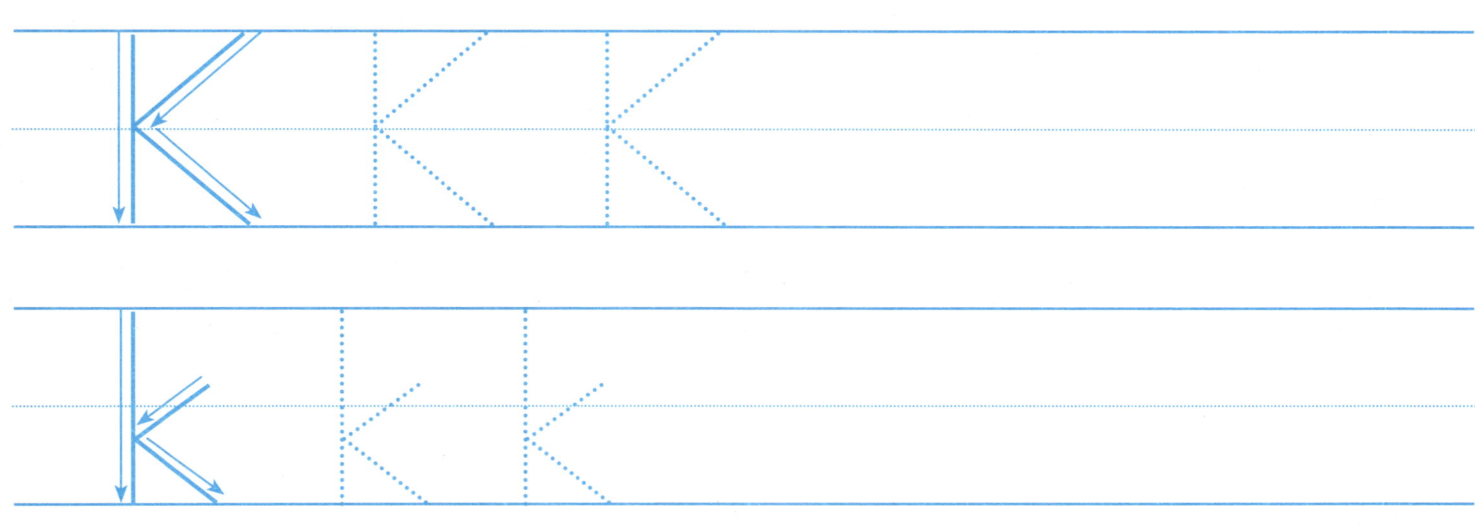

Tick (✓) all the objects the names of which begin with K.

Trace the word given below and colour the picture.

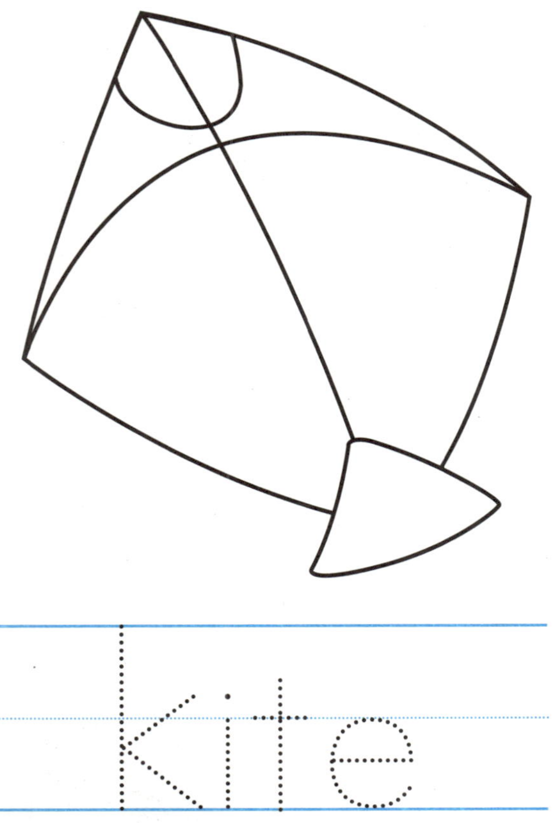

The Letter L

Write Ll with your pencil. Trace the dots first.

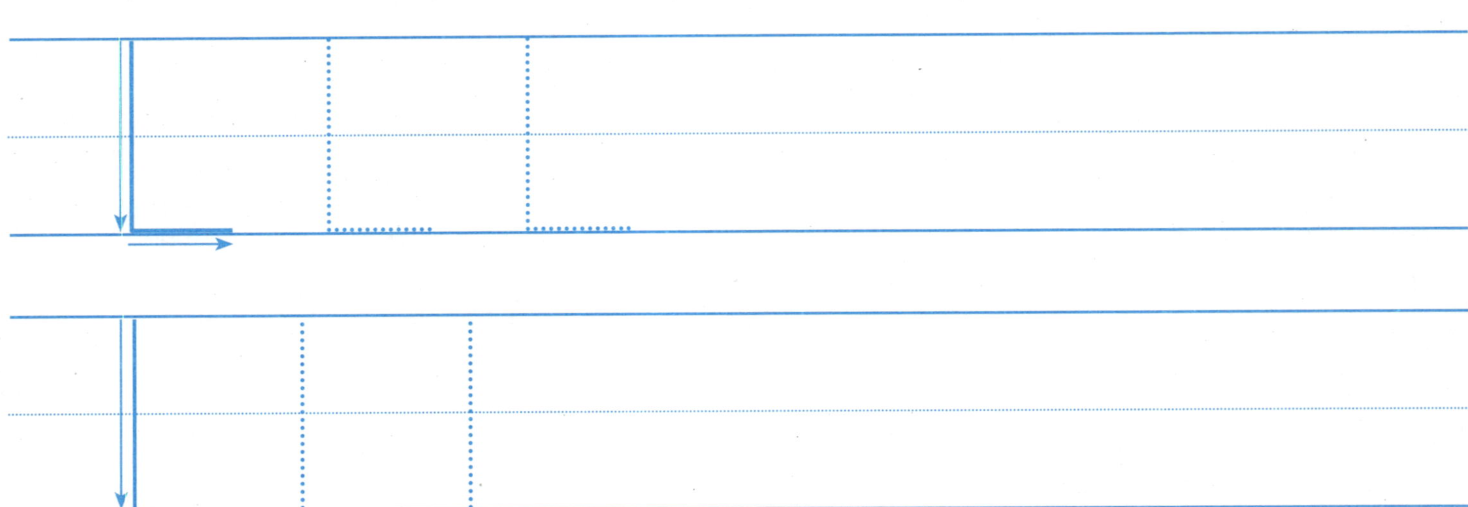

Help Leo, the cub, reach his home by following the objects that begin with L.

Trace the word given below and colour the picture.

Fun With Letters

Write the letter with which the picture words start.

Find and circle (O) the objects in the picture the names of which start with g, h and i.

How many did you find?

The Letter M

Write Mm with your pencil. Trace the dots first.

Draw a line from letter M to each object the name of which begins with M.

Trace the word given below and colour the picture.

mushroom

The Letter N

Write Nn with your pencil. Trace the dots first.

Colour all the objects the names of which begin with N.

Trace the word given below and colour the picture.

nest

The Letter O

Write Oo with your pencil. Trace the dots first.

How many Oos can you find in the picture? Circle (O) them all.

Trace the word given below and colour the picture.

orange

The Letter P

Write Pp with your pencil. Trace the dots first.

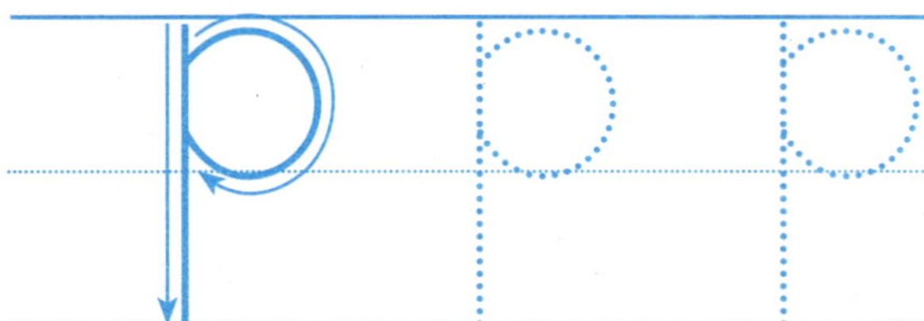

Fill in the blanks with P to complete each word. Join the dots and colour the objects.

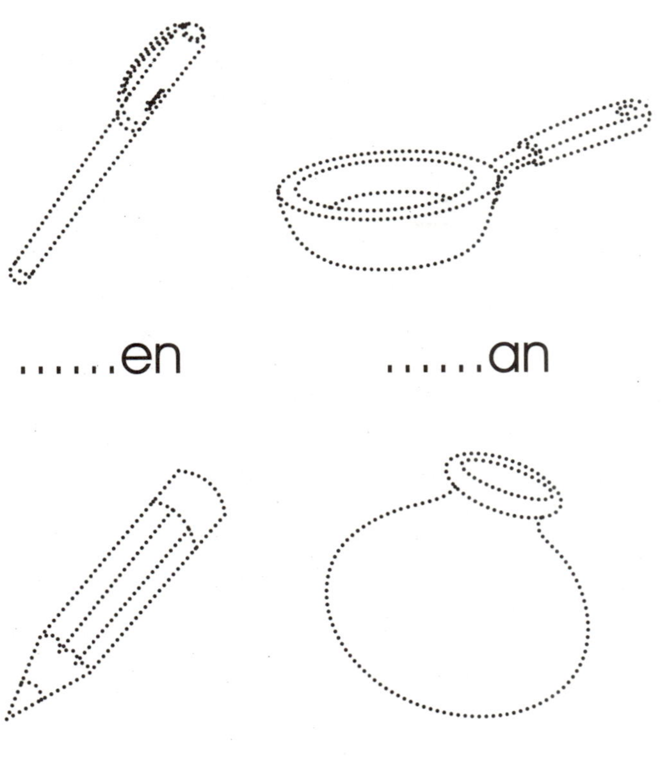

……en ……an

……encil ……ot

Trace the word given below and colour the picture.

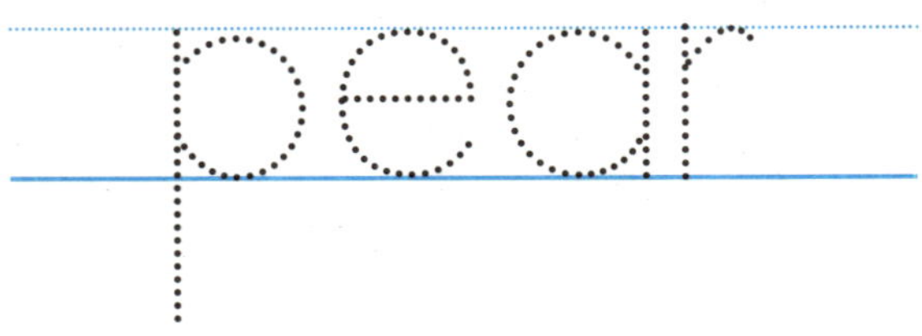

The Letter Q

Write Qq with your pencil. Trace the dots first.

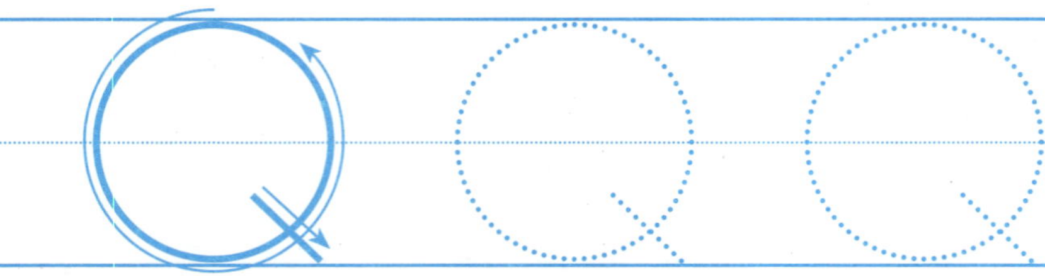

Circle (O) each object the name of which begins with Q.

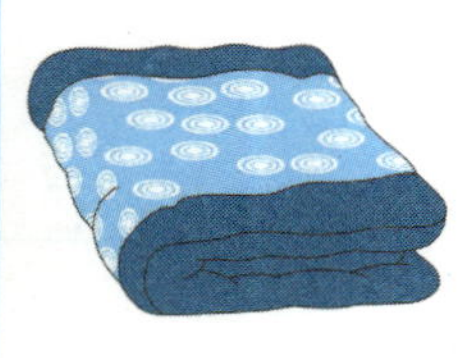

Trace the word given below and colour the picture.

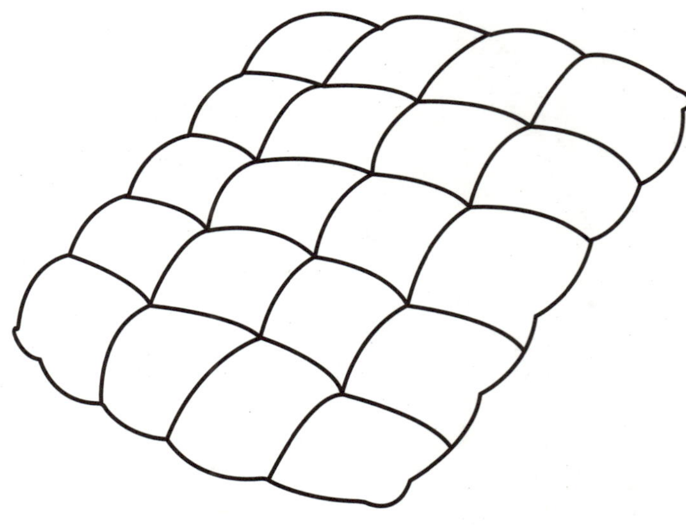

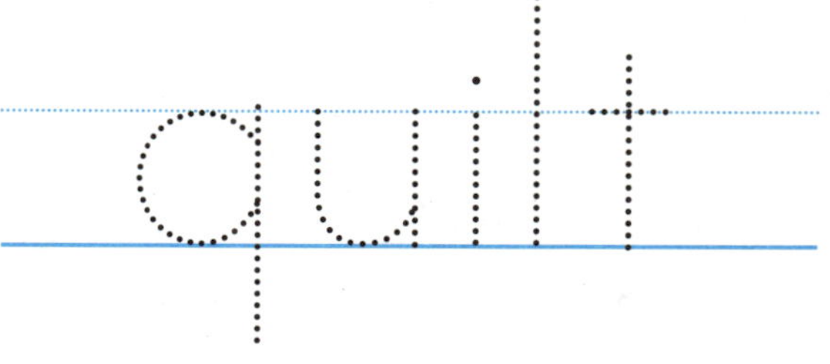

The Letter R

Write Rr with your pencil. Trace the dots first.

Can you name all the objects in the picture the names of which begin with R?

Trace the word given below and colour the picture.

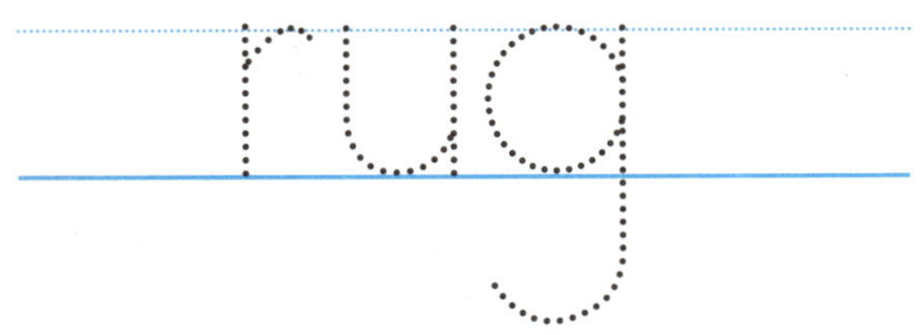

Fun With Letters

Draw lines from the objects in the picture to the letters with which their name begins.

Match the letters in uppercase with the lowercase letters by drawing lines.

M N O P Q R

o q m r n p

The Letter S

Write Ss with your pencil. Trace the dots first.

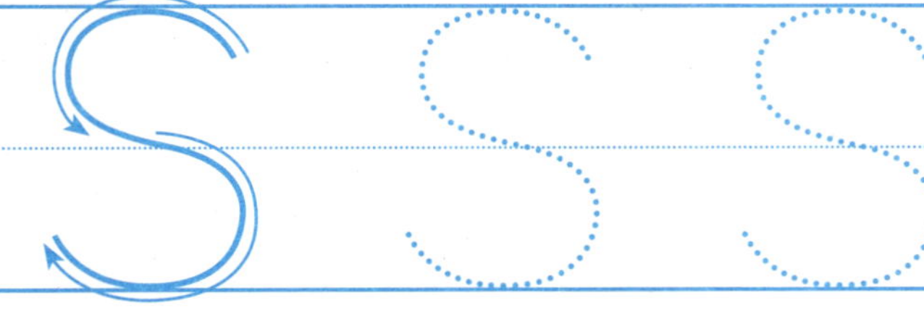

Tick (✓)all the objects in the picture the names of which begin with S.

Trace the word given below and colour the picture.

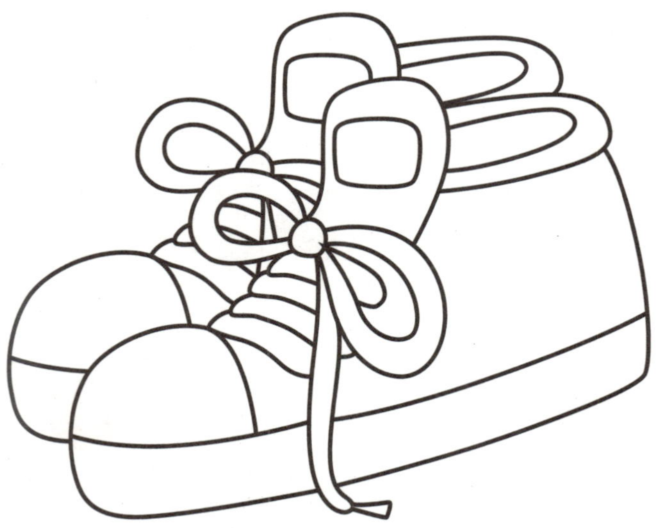

shoes

The Letter T

Write Tt with your pencil. Trace the dots first.

Help Tin, the turtle, to reach his home by following the objects the names of which begin with T.

Trace the word given below and colour the picture.

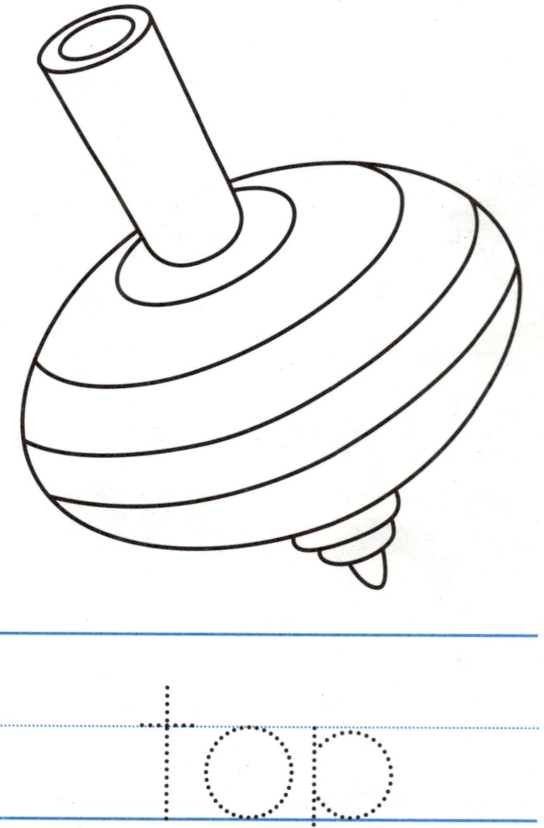

The Letter U

Write Uu with your pencil. Trace the dots first.

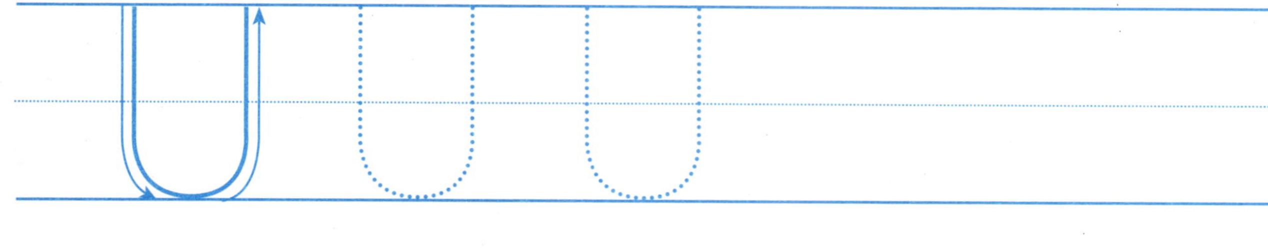

Draw a line from letter U to each object the name of which begins with U.

Trace the word given below and colour the picture.

umbrella

The Letter V

Write Vv with your pencil. Trace the dots first.

Colour all the objects the names of which begin with V.

Trace the word given below and colour the picture.

vase

The Letter W

Write Ww with your pencil. Trace the dots first.

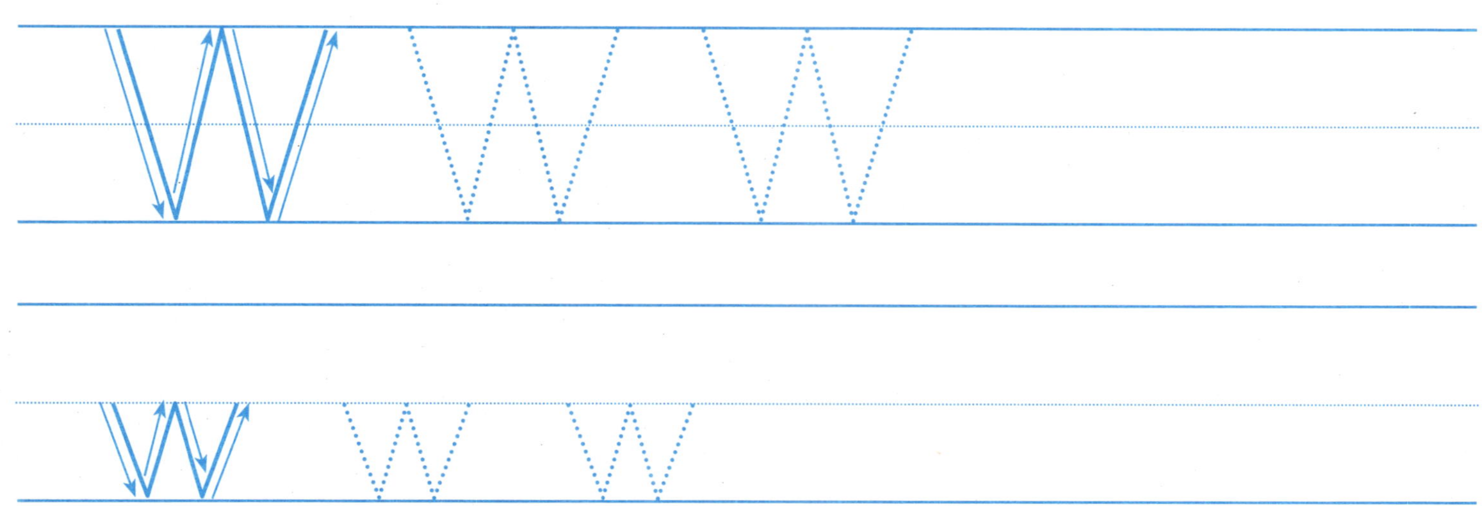

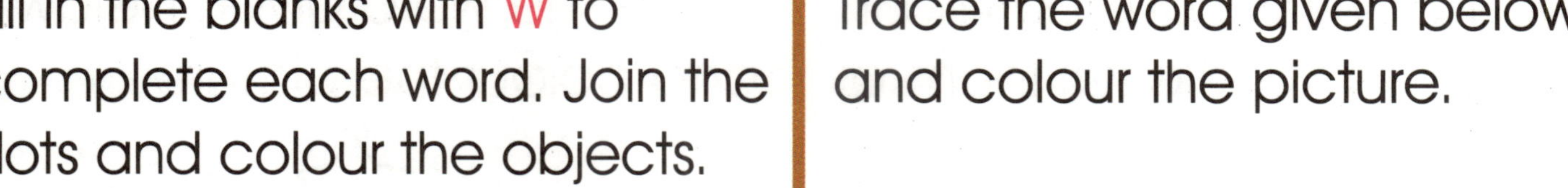

Fill in the blanks with W to complete each word. Join the dots and colour the objects.

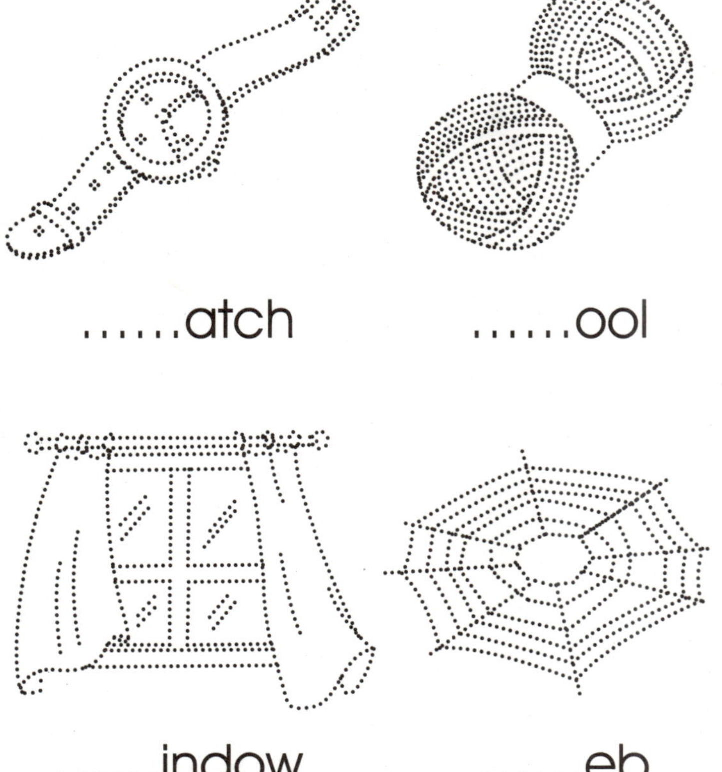

……atch

……ool

……indow

……eb

Trace the word given below and colour the picture.

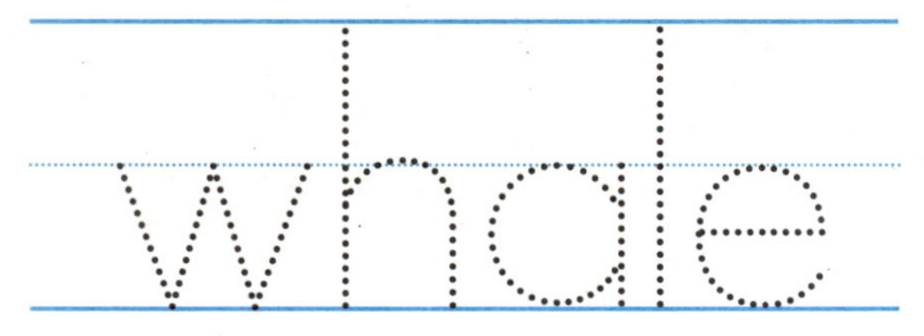

The Letter X

Write Xx with your pencil. Trace the dots first.

How many Xxs can you find in the picture? Circle (O) them all.

Trace the word given below and colour the picture.

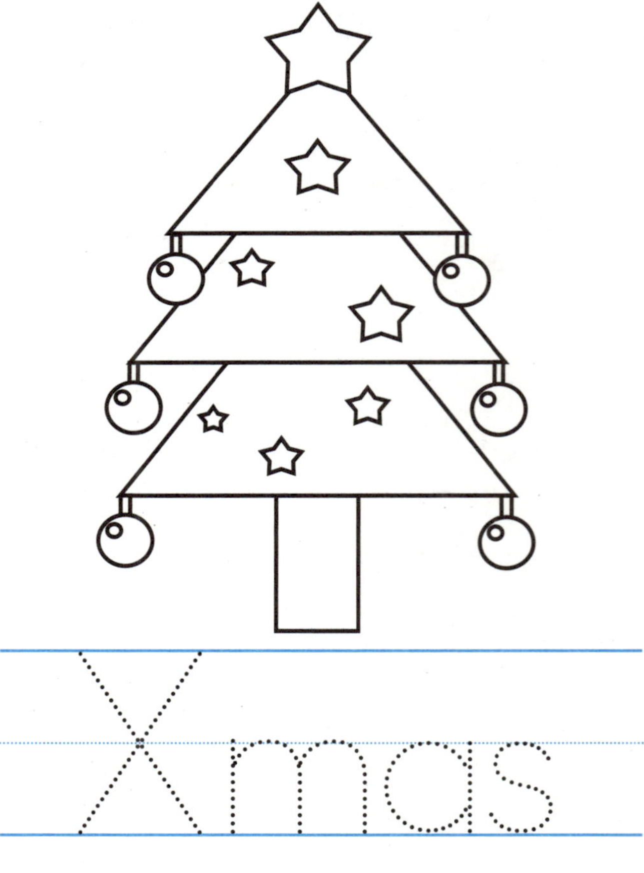

The Letter Y

Write Yy with your pencil. Trace the dots first.

Circle (O) all the objects the names of which begin with Y.

Trace the word given below and colour the picture.

The Letter Z

Write Zz with your pencil. Trace the dots first.

What is this place called? Can you spot an animal whose name begins with Z?

Trace the word given below and colour the picture.

Answer Key

Page 2
Page 3
Page 4
Page 5
Page 6
E
Page 7
Page 8
A D F
E C D
B F A
Page 9
Page 10
....hat
....hand
....hut
....hen
Page 11
Page 12
jet
juice
jug
jam
jar
joker
Page 13
Page 14
Page 15
L
J
K
g 4
h 1
i 1
Page 16
Page 17

Answer Key

Page 18

Page 19

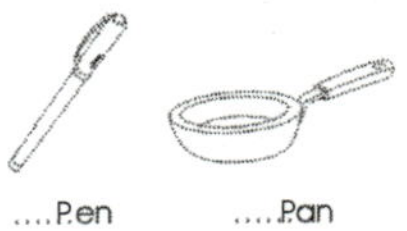

Page 20

Page 21

Page 22

Page 23

Page 24

Page 25

Page 26

Page 27

Page 28

Page 29

Page 30

Zoo, Zebra